I0415787

July 2012

DEBT LIMIT

Analysis of 2011-2012 Actions Taken and Effect of Delayed Increase on Borrowing Costs

G A O
Accountability * Integrity * Reliability

DEBT LIMIT

Analysis of 2011-2012 Actions Taken and Effect of Delayed Increase on Borrowing Costs

Highlights of GAO-12-701, a report to the Congress

Why GAO Did This Study

GAO previously examined challenges associated with managing cash and debt when delays in raising the debt limit occurred, focusing on the period from 1995 through 2010. In February 2011, GAO reported that delays in raising the debt limit create debt and cash challenges for Treasury, and these challenges have been exacerbated in recent years by a large growth in debt.

Delays in raising the debt limit occurred during 2011 and January 2012. GAO has prepared this report because of the nature of, and sensitivity toward, actions taken to manage federal debt during such delays. With regard to actions taken by Treasury during 2011 and January 2012 to manage federal debt when delays in raising the debt limit occurred, this report provides (1) a chronology of the significant events, (2) an analysis of whether actions taken by Treasury were consistent with legal authorities provided to manage federal debt during such delays, (3) an assessment of the extent to which Treasury restored uninvested principal and interest losses to federal government accounts in accordance with relevant legislation, and (4) an analysis of the effect that delays in raising the debt limit had on Treasury's borrowing costs and operations. To address these objectives, GAO reviewed Treasury correspondence and other documentation, analyzed Treasury and private security yield data, and interviewed Treasury officials. In commenting on GAO's draft report, Treasury broadly agreed with GAO's conclusions and provided technical comments, which GAO incorporated as appropriate.

View GAO-12-701. For more information, contact Gary T. Engel at (202) 512-3406 or engelg@gao.gov or Susan J. Irving at (202) 512-6806 or irvings@gao.gov.

What GAO Found

On August 2, 2011, Congress and the President enacted the Budget Control Act of 2011, which established a process that increased the debt limit to its current level of $16.4 trillion through incremental increases effective on August 2, 2011; after close of business on September 21, 2011; and after close of business on January 27, 2012. Delays in raising the debt limit occurred prior to the August 2011 and January 2012 increases, with the Department of the Treasury (Treasury) deviating from its normal debt management operations and taking a number of actions, referred to by Treasury as extraordinary actions, to avoid exceeding the debt limit.

The extraordinary actions Treasury took during 2011 and January 2012 to manage federal debt when delays in raising the debt limit occurred were consistent with relevant legislation and regulations. For 2011, these actions included suspending investments of the Civil Service Retirement and Disability Fund (CSRDF), the Postal Service Retiree Health Benefits Fund (Postal Benefits Fund), the Government Securities Investment Fund of the Federal Employees' Retirement System (G-Fund), and the Exchange Stabilization Fund (ESF), and redeeming certain investments held by the CSRDF earlier than normal. For January 2012, Treasury suspended investments to the G-Fund and ESF.

In accordance with relevant legislation, Treasury restored the uninvested principal and interest losses for 2011 and January 2012 to the CSRDF, Postal Benefits Fund, and G-Fund. Treasury also invested the uninvested principal for 2011 and January 2012 to the ESF. However, Treasury did not restore interest losses to the ESF because it lacks legislative authority to do so.

Delays in raising the debt limit can create uncertainty in the Treasury market and lead to higher Treasury borrowing costs. GAO estimated that delays in raising the debt limit in 2011 led to an increase in Treasury's borrowing costs of about $1.3 billion in fiscal year 2011. However, this does not account for the multiyear effects on increased costs for Treasury securities that will remain outstanding after fiscal year 2011. Further, according to Treasury officials, the increased focus on debt limit-related operations as such delays occurred required more time and Treasury resources and diverted Treasury's staff away from other important cash and debt management responsibilities.

The debt limit does not restrict Congress's ability to enact spending and revenue legislation that affects the level of debt or otherwise constrains fiscal policy; it restricts Treasury's authority to borrow to finance the decisions already enacted by Congress and the President. Congress also usually votes on increasing the debt limit after fiscal policy decisions affecting federal borrowing have begun to take effect. This approach to raising the debt limit does not facilitate debate over specific tax or spending proposals and their effect on debt. In February 2011, GAO reported, and continues to believe, that Congress should consider ways to better link decisions about the debt limit with decisions about spending and revenue to avoid potential disruptions to the Treasury market and to help inform the fiscal policy debate in a timely way.

_____ **United States Government Accountability Office**

Contents

Abbreviations

BCA	Budget Control Act of 2011
BPD	Bureau of the Public Debt
CM bills	cash management bills
CSRDF	Civil Service Retirement and Disability Fund
DISP	debt issuance suspension period
ESF	Exchange Stabilization Fund
FFB	Federal Financing Bank
FRED	Federal Reserve Economic Data
OFP	Office of Fiscal Projections
SLGS	State and Local Government Series
TIPS	Treasury Inflation-Protected Securities

GAO
Accountability * Integrity * Reliability

United States Government Accountability Office
Washington, DC 20548

July 23, 2012

Report to the Congress

Congress and the President have enacted laws to establish a limit on the amount of federal debt that can be outstanding at one time, referred to as the debt limit.[1] The debt limit does not restrict Congress's ability to enact spending and revenue legislation that affects the level of debt or otherwise constrains fiscal policy; it restricts the Department of the Treasury's (Treasury) authority to borrow to finance the decisions already enacted by Congress and the President. Congress also usually votes on increasing the debt limit after fiscal policy decisions affecting federal borrowing have begun to take effect. This approach to raising the debt limit does not facilitate debate over specific tax or spending proposals and their effect on debt. In addition, when delays in raising the debt limit occur, Treasury often must deviate from its normal cash and debt management operations and take a number of extraordinary actions to meet the government's obligations as they come due without exceeding the debt limit.[2]

We have previously examined challenges associated with managing cash and debt when delays in raising the debt limit occurred, focusing on the period from 1995 through 2010. We reported in February 2011 that delays in raising the debt limit create debt and cash management challenges for Treasury, and these challenges have been exacerbated in recent years by a large growth in debt.[3] The amount of borrowing capacity provided by taking the extraordinary actions available to Treasury has grown in size but has not kept pace with the growth in Treasury's borrowing needs. This means that once debt approaches the debt limit, Treasury may not be able to manage the amount of debt subject to the limit for as long a period of time as it had in the past before the debt limit must be increased. Further, failure to raise the debt limit in a timely manner could have serious negative consequences for the

---

[1]The debt limit is codified at 31 U.S.C. §§ 3101 and 3101A.

[2]Actions that are not part of Treasury's normal cash and debt management operations are considered "extraordinary actions" by Treasury.

[3]GAO, *Debt Limit: Delays Create Debt Management Challenges and Increase Uncertainty in the Treasury Market*, GAO-11-203 (Washington, D.C.: Feb. 22, 2011).

GAO-12-701 Debt Limit

Treasury market and increase borrowing costs. Managing debt when delays in raising the debt limit occur also diverts Treasury's resources away from other cash and debt management issues. In February 2011, we reported that Congress should consider ways to better link decisions about the debt limit with decisions about spending and revenue to avoid potential disruptions to the Treasury market and to help inform the fiscal policy debate in a timely way.

On January 6, 2011, the Secretary of the Treasury notified Congress that the debt limit would likely be reached between March 31, 2011, and May 16, 2011.[4] On August 2, 2011, Congress and the President enacted the Budget Control Act of 2011 (BCA),[5] which established a process that resulted in debt limit increases effective on August 2, 2011; after close of business on September 21, 2011; and after close of business on January 27, 2012.[6] Delays in raising the debt limit occurred prior to the August 2011 and January 2012 increases, with Treasury deviating from its normal debt management operations and taking a number of extraordinary actions to avoid exceeding the debt limit.

Because of the nature of, and sensitivity toward, actions taken to manage federal debt when delays in raising the debt limit occur, we prepared this report under the Comptroller General's authority to conduct evaluations on GAO's initiative to assist Congress with its oversight responsibilities. This report provides the results of our review of Treasury's actions during 2011 and January 2012 to manage federal debt when delays in raising the debt limit occurred. Specifically, the objectives of this report are to (1) provide a chronology of the significant events, (2) analyze whether actions taken by Treasury were consistent with legal authorities provided

---

[4]Treasury began using extraordinary actions on May 6, 2011.

[5]Pub. L. No. 112-25, § 301, 125 Stat. 240, 251 (Aug. 2, 2011), *codified at* 31 U.S.C. §§ 3101 and 3101A.

[6]Section 301 of the BCA provided for increases in the debt limit if the President certified that the debt subject to the limit was within $100 billion of the limit and that further borrowing was required to meet existing commitments subject to a joint congressional resolution of disapproval within the designated statutory time frames (see 31 U.S.C. §§ 3101A(a), (b)). The President provided his certifications to Congress, and the debt limit was increased upon the expiration of the statutory time frames for Congress's disapproval, after close of business on September 21, 2011, and January 27, 2012. However, additional borrowing pursuant to the increased debt limits did not occur until the next business days, which were September 22, 2011, and January 30, 2012, respectively.

to manage federal debt during such delays, (3) assess the extent to which Treasury restored uninvested principal and interest losses to federal government accounts in accordance with relevant legislation, and (4) analyze the effect that delays in raising the debt limit had on Treasury's borrowing costs and operations.

To answer the first three objectives, we reviewed Treasury correspondence, announcements, and documentation of the actions taken during 2011 and January 2012 to manage federal debt when delays in raising the debt limit occurred. We compared Treasury's actions to relevant legislation and regulations authorizing the specific extraordinary actions. We also reviewed documentation supporting uninvested principal, calculations of forgone interest, and the restoration of principal and interest losses. To evaluate whether Treasury followed normal investment and redemption policies and procedures for federal government accounts not affected by the extraordinary actions (e.g., Treasury's actions did not involve accounts that it is not authorized to use in such situations), we performed audit procedures over the investment and redemption activity of selected major accounts.

To determine what effect delays in raising the debt limit in 2011 had on Treasury's borrowing costs, we performed a multivariate regression analysis of the daily yield spread—yields on private securities minus yields on Treasury securities of comparable maturities—during the debt limit event period.[7] We used yield spreads during the 3-month pre-event period as a benchmark against which yield spreads during the event period were compared. We also examined changes in the yield spread during the January 2012 debt limit event period. See appendix II for more details on how we estimated increased borrowing costs, including limitations to our using a multivariate regression to measure changes in Treasury's borrowing costs attributable to delays in raising the debt limit.[8] We obtained Treasury auction data for this analysis from Treasury and private security yields and other data from the Federal Reserve Bank of St. Louis's Federal Reserve Economic Data (FRED) source. We also

---

[7]For the purposes of our analysis, a debt limit event period begins when Treasury first warns of the need to raise the debt limit and ends when legislation to raise the limit takes effect. For 2011, the debt limit event period was from January 6, 2011, through August 1, 2011.

[8]App. II also discusses differences with previous analyses, which focused on short-term Treasury securities.

used data on Standard & Poor's 500 total return index from IHS Global Insight in our analysis. To assess the reliability of these data, we looked for outliers and anomalies. These databases are commonly used by Treasury and researchers to examine the Treasury market and related transactions. On the basis of our assessment, we believe the data are sufficiently reliable for the purpose of this review. We also reviewed documents provided by Treasury, interviewed Treasury officials, and obtained estimates from Treasury of the number of personnel and amount of time involved in Treasury's efforts to manage federal debt during such delays. We reviewed these estimates for reasonableness.

We conducted this performance audit from May 2011 to July 2012 in accordance with generally accepted government auditing standards. Those standards require that we plan and perform the audit to obtain sufficient, appropriate evidence to provide a reasonable basis for our findings and conclusions based on our audit objectives. We believe that the evidence obtained provides a reasonable basis for our findings and conclusions based on our audit objectives. See appendixes I and II for more details on our objectives, scope, and methodology.

Background

Congress and the President first enacted a statutory limit on federal debt during World War I to eliminate the need for Congress to approve each new debt issuance and provide Treasury with greater discretion over how it finances the government's day-to-day borrowing needs. With the Public Debt Act of 1941,[9] Congress and the President set an overall limit of $65 billion on Treasury debt obligations that could be outstanding at any one time and since then have enacted a number of debt limit increases. Most recently, Congress and the President enacted the BCA, which established a process that resulted in debt limit increases in three increments—$400 billion in August 2011, $500 billion in September 2011, and $1,200 billion in January 2012—for a total increase of $2.1 trillion, raising the debt limit to $16.394 trillion. As shown in figure 1, the amount of reported outstanding debt subject to the limit has increased from $5,137 billion on September 30, 1996, to $15,730 billion on May 31, 2012.

---

[9]Pub. L. No. 77-7, 55 Stat. 7 (Feb. 19, 1941).

Figure 1: Debt Subject to the Limit, September 30, 1996, through September 30, 2011, and May 31, 2012

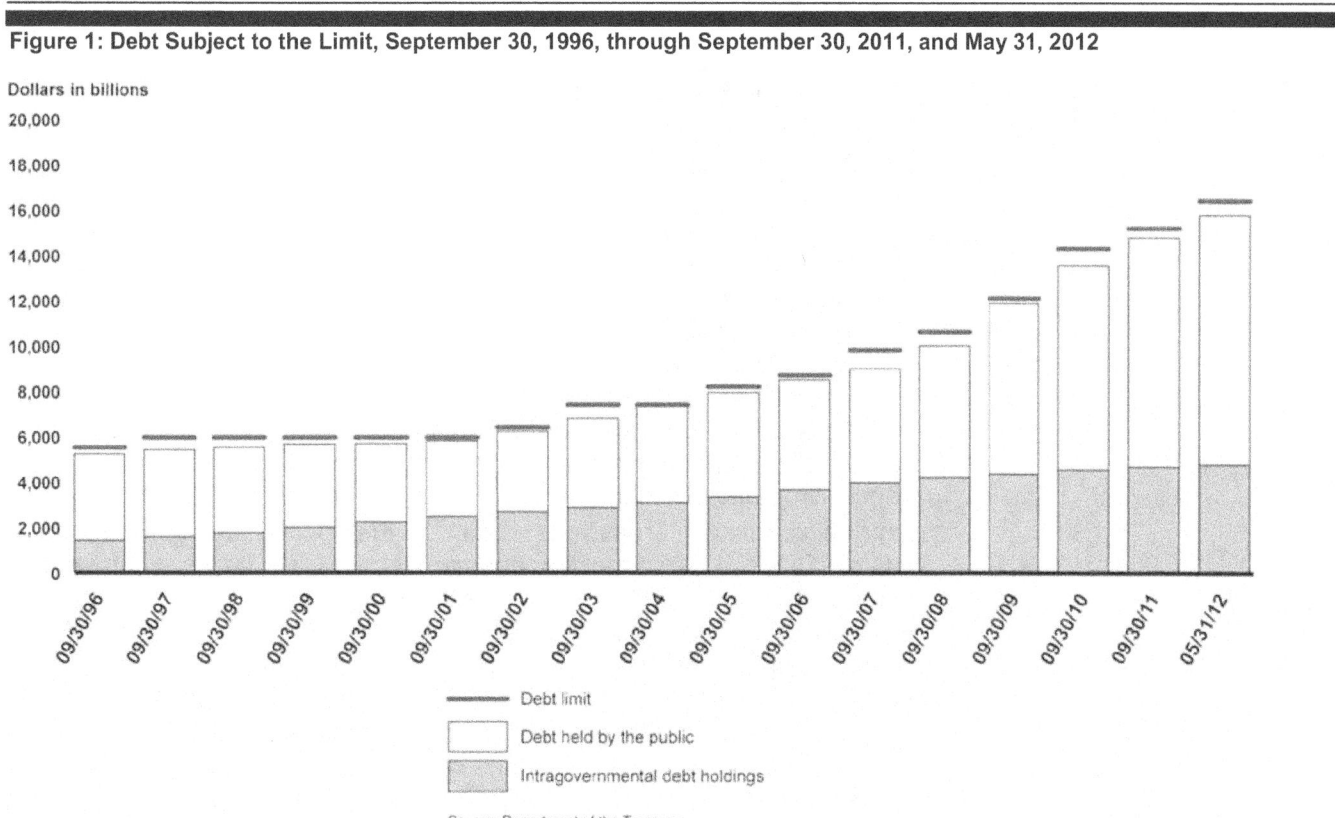

Source: Department of the Treasury

Debt subject to the limit includes both debt held by the public and intragovernmental debt holdings. Debt held by the public consists primarily of marketable Treasury securities, such as bonds, notes, bills, cash management bills (CM bills), and Treasury Inflation-Protected Securities (TIPS), which are sold through auctions and can be resold by whoever owns them.[10] Treasury also issues a smaller amount of nonmarketable securities, such as savings securities and special securities for state and local governments. Debt held by the public primarily represents the amount the federal government has borrowed to

---

[10]CM bills are flexible securities that Treasury issues outside of its regular preannounced auction schedule. Treasury sets the amount and time to maturity to meet its immediate borrowing needs at the time. TIPS are inflation-indexed securities that unlike nominal securities offer inflation protection to investors who are willing to pay a premium for this protection in the form of lower interest rates.

finance cumulative cash deficits. Intragovernmental debt holdings represent balances of Treasury securities held in federal government accounts, such as the Social Security and Medicare trust funds. Intragovernmental debt increases when these accounts run a surplus or accrue interest on existing securities.[11]

The Secretary of the Treasury has several responsibilities related to the federal government's financial management operations. These include paying the government's obligations and investing the excess annual receipts (including interest earnings) over disbursements of federal government accounts with investment authority. To meet these responsibilities, the Secretary of the Treasury is authorized by law to issue the necessary securities to federal government accounts with investment authority for investment purposes and to borrow the necessary funds from the public to pay government obligations.[12] Under normal conditions, Treasury is notified by the appropriate agency (such as the Office of Personnel Management for the Civil Service Retirement and Disability Fund (CSRDF)) of the amount that should be invested on its behalf, and Treasury then makes the investment. In some cases, the actual security that Treasury should purchase is also specified. When a federal government account with investment authority needs to make disbursements, Treasury is normally notified of the amount of securities that need to be redeemed. In some cases, Treasury is also notified to redeem specific securities. The Treasury securities issued to federal government accounts with investment authority count against the debt limit. If these accounts' receipts are not invested, the amount of debt subject to the limit does not increase.

---

[11]A very small amount of total federal debt is not subject to the debt limit. This amount is primarily composed of unamortized discounts on Treasury bills and Zero Coupon Treasury bonds; debt securities issued by agencies other than Treasury, such as the Tennessee Valley Authority; and debt securities issued by the Federal Financing Bank. As of September 30, 2011, 99.5 percent of federal debt was subject to the debt limit.

[12]The majority of securities held by federal government accounts are Government Account Series (GAS) securities. GAS securities consist of par value securities and market-based securities, with terms ranging from on demand out to 30 years. Par value securities are issued and redeemed at par (100 percent of face value), regardless of current market conditions. Market-based securities, however, can be issued at a premium or discount and are redeemed at par value on the maturity date or at market value if redeemed before the maturing date.

Under normal circumstances, the debt limit is not an impediment to carrying out these investment responsibilities. However, when federal debt is near or at the debt limit, increasing the debt limit frequently involves lengthy debate by Congress. When delays occur, Treasury has to depart from normal cash and debt management operations to avoid exceeding the debt limit. In 1986 and 1987, after Treasury's experiences during prior debt limit crises, Congress authorized the Secretary of the Treasury to use the CSRDF and the Government Securities Investment Fund of the Federal Employees' Retirement System (G-Fund) to help Treasury manage federal debt when delays in raising the debt limit occur. Treasury has also taken other actions in the past to manage federal debt during such delays. Table 1 provides an overview of each action.

Table 1: Extraordinary Actions Available to Treasury to Manage Debt When Delays in Raising the Debt Limit Occur

Extraordinary action	Description of extraordinary action
Suspension of new issuances and conversion of demand deposit securities to special 90-day certificates of indebtedness of State and Local Government Series (SLGS) securities	SLGS securities are special securities offered to state and local governments and other issuers of tax-exempt bonds. Suspending new SLGS issuances reduces uncertainty over future increases in debt subject to the limit but eliminates a flexible, low-cost option that state and local government issuers have frequently used when refinancing their existing debt before maturity. Converting SLGS demand deposit securities, which increase daily for the interest earned, to special 90-day certificates of indebtedness, which pay interest separately, results in debt subject to the limit not increasing daily for the interest earned.
Exchanging Federal Financing Bank (FFB) debt for debt subject to the limit	FFB is a government corporation under the general supervision and direction of the Secretary of the Treasury, which borrows from the Treasury to finance purchases of agency debt and agency guaranteed debt. It can also issue up to $15 billion of its own debt—FFB 9(a) obligations—that is not subject to the debt limit. This debt can be exchanged with other federal debt (e.g., securities held by the CSRDF) to reduce the amount of debt subject to the limit.
Suspension of investments to the Government Securities Investment Fund of the Federal Employees' Retirement System (G-Fund)[a]	The G-Fund contains contributions made by federal employees toward their retirement as part of the Thrift Savings Plan program, which are invested in one-day nonmarketable Treasury securities that are subject to the debt limit. If the Secretary determines that the G-Fund may not be fully invested without exceeding the debt limit, Treasury can suspend investments for the entire amount or a portion of the G-Fund on a daily basis to reduce debt subject to the limit. Treasury must notify Congress in writing when the G-Fund cannot be fully invested without exceeding the debt limit. Treasury is required to make the G-Fund whole after the debt limit has been increased.
Suspension of Exchange Stabilization Fund (ESF) investments	The ESF is used to help provide a stable system of monetary exchange rates. Dollar-denominated assets of the ESF not used for program purposes are generally invested in one-day nonmarketable Treasury securities that are subject to the debt limit. When debt approaches the limit, Treasury can suspend investment for the entire amount or a portion of the ESF's maturing nonmarketable Treasury securities. Treasury lacks legislative authority to restore lost interest to the ESF when the debt limit is increased.
Suspension of new investments to the Civil Service Retirement and Disability Trust Fund (CSRDF) and Postal Service Retiree Health Benefits Fund (Postal Benefits Fund)[b]	Contributions into the CSRDF (by federal government agencies and their civilian employees toward retirement benefits) and Postal Benefits Fund (by the United States Postal Service toward its retirees' health benefits) are invested in par value nonmarketable Treasury securities that are subject to the debt limit. Treasury is able to suspend new investments to the CSRDF and Postal Benefits Fund if the investment cannot be made without exceeding the debt limit. Treasury must notify Congress in writing when the CSRDF cannot be fully invested without exceeding the debt limit. Treasury is required to make the CSRDF and Postal Benefits Fund whole after the debt issuance suspension period (DISP)—a period in which Treasury determines that it cannot issue debt without exceeding the debt limit—has ended.
Disinvestment of securities held by the CSRDF and Postal Benefits Fund[c]	Treasury is able to disinvest (e.g., redeem earlier than normal) Treasury securities held by the CSRDF and Postal Benefits Fund to prevent the amount of debt from exceeding the debt limit. Treasury must determine that a DISP exists and the length of the DISP, which Treasury uses to determine the amount of investments that can be disinvested. Treasury also must notify Congress in writing when the CSRDF cannot be fully invested without exceeding the debt limit. Treasury is required to make the CSRDF and Postal Benefits Fund whole after the DISP has ended.

Source: GAO analysis of related legislation and regulations.

[a] 5 U.S.C. §§ 8438(g), (h).

[b] 5 U.S.C. §§ 8348(j), (l) and 5 U.S.C. § 8909a(c).

[c] 5 U.S.C. §§ 8348(k), (l) and 5 U.S.C. § 8909a(c).

We have previously reported on aspects of Treasury's actions during the 2003 and 2002 debt issuance suspension periods (DISP), and the 1995-1996 and other debt limit crises.[13]

Chronology of Events

In January 2011, Treasury determined that the debt limit of $14.294 trillion set in February 2010 would likely be reached by May 16, 2011. In May 2011, Treasury determined that it was necessary to use extraordinary actions to manage federal debt during the delay in raising the debt limit, which lasted through August 1, 2011. Treasury again determined that extraordinary actions were needed to manage federal debt in January 2012. Table 2 shows the significant events from January 6, 2011, through January 30, 2012, that relate to the debt limit.

Table 2: Chronology of Events Related to the Debt Limit, January 2011 through January 2012

Date	Event
Events leading up to the use of extraordinary actions in 2011	
January 6, 2011	The Secretary of the Treasury sent a letter to the Senate Majority Leader requesting an increase in the debt limit. The letter stated that the debt limit would likely be reached sometime between March 31, 2011, and May 16, 2011.
April 4, 2011	The Secretary of the Treasury sent a letter to the Senate and House Majority and Minority Leaders stating that Treasury's updated estimates indicated that the debt limit would be reached no later than May 16, 2011. The letter projected that Treasury's borrowing authority using available extraordinary measures would be exhausted after about July 8, 2011.
May 2, 2011	The Secretary of the Treasury sent a letter to the Senate and House Majority and Minority Leaders indicating that Treasury would begin suspending the issuance of SLGS securities on May 6, 2011, and if Congress had not increased the debt limit by May 16, 2011, Treasury would take further extraordinary actions beginning on that date. Treasury stated that these actions would extend Treasury's borrowing authority until about August 2, 2011.
Extraordinary actions in 2011	
May 6, 2011	Treasury began suspending new issuances of SLGS securities and converted all outstanding SLGS demand deposit securities to special 90-day certificates of indebtedness.
May 16, 2011	The Secretary of the Treasury notified Congress that he had determined a DISP existed from May 16, 2011, until August 2, 2011, and Treasury
	(1) redeemed a portion of investments held by the CSRDF earlier than normal and
	(2) began suspending new investments to the CSRDF.
	The Secretary of the Treasury notified Congress that he would be unable to fully invest the G-Fund and Treasury began suspending investments to the G-Fund.

---

[13]GAO products related to federal debt and debt management, including the debt limit, can be found at http://www.gao.gov/special.pubs/longterm/past/#debt.

Date	Event
June 30, 2011	Treasury suspended new investments to the Postal Benefits Fund.
July 15, 2011	Treasury began suspending investments to the ESF.
Events to raise the debt limit and restore principal and interest in 2011	
August 2, 2011	As authorized by the BCA, the debt limit increased $400 billion to $14.694 trillion.
	Treasury invested all uninvested principal of the CSRDF, Postal Benefits Fund, G-Fund, and ESF.
	Treasury resumed the sale of SLGS securities and converted the special 90-day certificates of indebtedness back to demand deposits including accrued interest.
August 3, 2011	Treasury restored interest losses incurred by the G-Fund.
After close of business on September 21, 2011	As authorized by the BCA, the debt limit increased $500 billion to $15.194 trillion.
December 30, 2011	Treasury restored interest losses incurred by the CSRDF and the Postal Benefits Fund.
Extraordinary actions in January 2012	
January 4, 2012	Treasury began suspending investments to the ESF.
January 17, 2012	The Secretary of the Treasury notified Congress that he would be unable to fully invest the G-Fund and Treasury began suspending investments to the G-Fund.
Events to raise the debt limit and restore principal and interest in January 2012	
After close of business on January 27, 2012	As authorized by the BCA, the debt limit increased $1.2 trillion to $16.394 trillion.
January 30, 2012	Treasury invested all uninvested principal of the G-Fund and ESF and restored interest losses incurred by the G-Fund.

Source: GAO analysis of congressional actions and documentation from Treasury.

Extraordinary Actions to Manage Debt Were Consistent with Legislation and Regulations

The extraordinary actions Treasury took during 2011 and January 2012 to manage federal debt when delays in raising the debt limit occurred were consistent with relevant authorizing legislation and regulations. These actions related to State and Local Government Series (SLGS) securities, and the CSRDF, Postal Service Retiree Health Benefits Fund (Postal Benefits Fund), G-Fund, and Exchange Stabilization Fund (ESF). For other major federal government accounts with investment authority, Treasury used its normal investment and redemption policies and procedures to handle receipts and maturing investments and to redeem Treasury securities.

Actions Related to SLGS Securities

Treasury took the first extraordinary action on May 6, 2011, by suspending new issuances of SLGS securities.[14] Prior to the suspension, the reported amount of SLGS securities outstanding was about $177.3 billion. This level declined to a reported amount of about $146.5 billion by August 1, 2011. On August 2, 2011, Treasury resumed the sale of SLGS securities. Treasury also converted SLGS demand deposit securities outstanding on May 6, 2011, to special 90-day certificates of indebtedness. On August 2, 2011, Treasury converted the special 90-day certificates of indebtedness back to demand deposits including accrued interest. Treasury maintained spreadsheets to track the certificates of indebtedness and the daily interest accruals. Treasury's actions related to the SLGS demand deposit securities were in accordance with 31 C.F.R. Part 344.7 (b), which authorizes the Secretary of the Treasury to invest any unredeemed SLGS demand deposit securities in special 90-day certificates of indebtedness. Treasury did not use its authority to suspend new issuances of or convert SLGS securities during January 2012.

Actions Related to the CSRDF

The Secretary of the Treasury notified Congress that he had determined that a DISP existed for the CSRDF on May 16, 2011, after concluding that he would not be able to issue debt securities without exceeding the debt limit. On that day, Treasury redeemed certain investments held by the CSRDF earlier than normal and began suspending new investments of CSRDF receipts. Treasury did not use its authority to redeem or suspend investments of the CSRDF during January 2012.

Early Redemption of Securities Held by the CSRDF

Subsection 8348(k) of title 5, United States Code, authorizes the Secretary of the Treasury to redeem securities or other invested assets of the CSRDF before maturity to prevent the amount of debt from exceeding the debt limit. The statute does not require that early redemptions be made only for the purpose of making CSRDF payments. Further, the statute permits early redemptions even if the CSRDF has adequate cash balances to cover such payments. However, the statute provides that the amount redeemed may not exceed the total amount of the payments authorized to be made from the CSRDF during the DISP.

---

[14]Treasury announced that subscriptions for SLGS securities received before noon Eastern Daylight Time on May 6, 2011, would be honored.

Treasury decided to redeem securities held by the CSRDF earlier than normal in accordance with subsection 8348(k)(1) of title 5, United States Code. To take such action, the Secretary of the Treasury must determine that a DISP exists and the length of the DISP. The statute authorizing the DISP and its legislative history are silent as to how to determine the length of a DISP. On May 16, 2011, the Secretary of the Treasury notified Congress that a DISP, as it relates to the CSRDF, would begin that day and would last through August 2, 2011.

On May 16, 2011, Treasury redeemed about $17.1 billion of securities held by the CSRDF before maturity using its authority under subsection 8348(k)(1) of title 5, United States Code. The $17.1 billion redemption amount was determined based on (1) the length of the DISP (May 16, 2011, through August 2, 2011) and (2) the estimated monthly CSRDF benefit payments and expenses that would occur during that time.[15] These were appropriate factors to use in determining the amount of Treasury securities held by the CSRDF to redeem early.

From May 16, 2011, through July 31, 2011, about $11.8 billion of actual benefit payments and expenses occurred, leaving about $5.3 billion of uninvested principal from the $17.1 billion that had been redeemed early. On August 1, 2011, benefit payments were about $5.7 billion. As such, Treasury redeemed only the approximate $0.4 billion difference between the $5.3 billion uninvested principal amount and the actual amount of benefit payments to be made.

Suspension of New Investments to the CSRDF

Subsection 8348(j)(1) of title 5, United States Code, authorizes the Secretary of the Treasury to suspend additional investment of amounts in the CSRDF if the investment cannot be made without exceeding the debt limit. From May 16, 2011, through August 1, 2011, Treasury suspended about $86 billion of investments to the CSRDF. Of this amount, $63.1 billion related to securities that matured on June 30, 2011, and were to be reinvested; $17.4 billion was from the semiannual interest payment on June 30, 2011; and $5.5 billion represented cash receipts.

---

[15]CSRDF benefit payments and expenses for May through August 2011 were estimated to be approximately $5.9 billion monthly, with the majority occurring on the first business day of the month.

Actions Related to the Postal Benefits Fund	Subsection 8909a(c) of title 5, United States Code, requires investments to be made for the Postal Benefits Fund in the same manner as investments for the CSRDF under section 8348. This includes the provisions authorizing the early redemption and suspension of investments. As discussed above for the CSRDF, the amount redeemed earlier than normal may not exceed the total amount of the payments authorized to be made during the DISP. Subsection 8906(g)(2)(A) of title 5, United States Code, authorizes payments to be made from the Postal Benefits Fund beginning after September 30, 2016. As such, Treasury did not redeem investments of the Postal Benefits Fund earlier than normal during 2011 and January 2012. On June 30, 2011, Treasury suspended about $9.5 billion of new investments to the Postal Benefits Fund. Of this amount, $8.7 billion related to securities that matured on June 30, 2011, and were to be reinvested, and $0.8 billion was from the semiannual interest payment on June 30, 2011. Treasury did not use its authority to suspend investments of the Postal Benefits Fund during January 2012.
Actions Related to the G-Fund	Subsection 8438(g)(1) of title 5, United States Code, authorizes the Secretary of the Treasury to suspend the issuance of additional amounts of investments to the G-Fund if the issuance cannot be made without causing the debt limit to be exceeded. On most days from May 16, 2011, through August 1, 2011, and each day from January 17, 2012, through January 27, 2012, Treasury did not fully invest the holdings of the G-Fund. Since the G-Fund invests in one-day securities that are redeemed and reinvested each business day, the amount of uninvested principal varied most days depending on the federal government's outstanding debt. Although Treasury can accurately predict the outcome of some events that affect the outstanding debt, it cannot precisely determine the outcome of others until they occur. For example, the amount of Treasury securities that Treasury will issue to the public from an auction can be determined some days in advance because Treasury can control the amount that will be issued. On the other hand, the amount of savings bonds that will be issued and redeemed and the amount of Treasury securities that will be issued to, or redeemed by, various federal government accounts with investment authority are difficult to precisely predict. Because of these difficulties, Treasury needed to ensure that the normal investment and redemption activities associated with Treasury securities did not cause the debt limit to be exceeded while also

maintaining normal investment and redemption policies for the majority of these accounts. To accomplish these objectives, for each day of the above-noted periods, Treasury

- calculated the amount of debt subject to the limit, excluding the receipts that the G-Fund would normally invest;
- determined the amount of G-Fund receipts that could safely be invested without exceeding the debt limit and invested this amount in Treasury securities; and
- suspended investment, when necessary, of the G-Fund's remaining receipts.

As of August 1, 2011, the business day prior to the debt limit increase, the G-Fund had approximately $137.5 billion available for suspension, with the entire amount suspended as of that date. As of January 27, 2012, the business day prior to the debt limit increase, the G-Fund had approximately $147.6 billion available for suspension, with about $36.9 billion suspended as of that date.

Actions Related to the ESF

The purpose of the ESF is to help provide a stable system of monetary exchange rates. The law establishing the ESF authorizes the Secretary of the Treasury to invest the ESF's balances not needed for program purposes in Treasury securities. Section 5302 of title 31, United States Code, authorizes the Secretary of the Treasury to determine when, and if, excess funds for the ESF will be invested. On several occasions from July 15, 2011, through August 1, 2011, and each day from January 4, 2012, through January 27, 2012, Treasury did not fully invest the dollar-denominated portion of the ESF in Treasury securities. Since the ESF invests the dollar-denominated portion of the fund in one-day Treasury securities that are redeemed and reinvested each business day, the amount of uninvested principal varied several days, depending on the federal government's outstanding debt. For each day, Treasury determined the amount of funds that the ESF would be allowed to invest in Treasury securities and, when necessary, suspended some investments of the ESF receipts and maturing securities that would have caused the debt limit to be exceeded. The process discussed above for the G-Fund was also used for the ESF. During the 2011 period, the ESF had approximately $22.8 billion available for suspension, with about $6.9 billion of this amount suspended as of August 1, 2011, the business day prior to the debt limit increase. During January 2012, the ESF had approximately $22.7 billion available for suspension, with the entire amount suspended as of January 17, 2012. The entire amount continued to be suspended each day through January 27, 2012, the business day prior to the debt limit increase.

As a result of an error in calculating debt subject to the limit from November 2, 2011, through December 29, 2011, Treasury suspended an incorrect amount from the ESF from January 4, 2012, through January 10, 2012. A programming change to Treasury's debt accounting system caused an incorrect calculation of unamortized discounts on Treasury bills to be subtracted from total debt outstanding in calculating debt subject to the limit.[16] Treasury identified the error during a contingency operation on December 29, 2011. At that time, the cumulative effect of the error was $181 million. The error in the program was corrected immediately; however, the adjustment to correct the $181 million was not recorded until January 11, 2012.[17]

Debt subject to the limit was sufficiently below the debt limit from November 2, 2011, through January 3, 2012, such that if the error was taken into account, debt subject to the limit would still have been below the debt limit. Treasury began using the ESF to manage federal debt during the delay in raising the debt limit on January 4, 2012. To determine whether Treasury would have exceeded the debt limit from January 4, 2012, through January 10, 2012, absent this error, we reviewed the invested balances of the ESF during this period. Based on our review, we found that the ESF had sufficient invested balances that could have been used to manage federal debt during the delay. For example, as of January 10, 2012, cumulative investments totaling $12.306 billion had been suspended from the ESF. If the error had not occurred, cumulative investments totaling $12.487 billion would have been suspended from the ESF, $181 million more than what was actually suspended, but well below the approximate $22.7 billion available for suspension. Therefore, Treasury would have been able to suspend additional investments from the ESF to remain under the debt limit. As a result of overinvesting the ESF from January 4, 2012, through January 10, 2012, Treasury also

---

[16]Treasury bills are usually issued at a discount from the face value, but may also be issued at par. The discounts are amortized (or expensed) over the term of the securities with the amount yet to be amortized referred to as the unamortized discount.

[17]While Treasury identified the source of the error on December 29, 2011, additional research was required to determine the period of the error and the amount involved.

overpaid interest to the ESF during this period. Treasury corrected the interest paid by making an adjustment of $402.63 on January 11, 2012.

Normal Investment and Redemption Policies Used on Major Federal Government Accounts with Investment Authority

We analyzed major federal government accounts with investment authority for which Treasury stated it had followed its normal investment and redemption policies and procedures during the periods from May 16, 2011, through August 1, 2011, and from January 4, 2012, through January 27, 2012, to manage federal debt when delays in raising the debt limit occurred.[18] Our analysis was intended to verify that Treasury's actions to manage federal debt during such delays did not involve federal government accounts that Treasury is not authorized to use in such situations. We found that for all the accounts we reviewed, Treasury used its normal investment and redemption policies and procedures to handle receipts and maturing investments and to redeem Treasury securities. Table 3 lists the federal government accounts with investment authority included in our analysis.

---

[18]Our analysis focused on accounts with reported balances as of April 30, 2011, and December 31, 2011, of Treasury securities greater than $10 billion.

Table 3: Reported Balances as of April 30, 2011, and December 31, 2011, of Treasury Securities Held by Selected Major Federal Government Accounts with Investment Authority

Dollars in billions

Federal government accounts with investment authority[a]	Treasury securities held as of April 30, 2011[b]	Treasury securities held as of December 31, 2011[b]
SSA: Federal Old-Age and Survivors Insurance Trust Fund[c]	$2,450	$2,525
OPM: Civil Service Retirement and Disability Fund	[d]	803[e]
DOD: Military Retirement Fund	335	383
HHS: Federal Hospital Insurance Trust Fund[f]	261	244
SSA: Federal Disability Insurance Trust Fund[c]	173	154
DOD: DOD Medicare-Eligible Retiree Health Care Fund	161	177
HHS: Federal Supplementary Medical Insurance Trust Fund[f]	72	80
DOE: Nuclear Waste Disposal Fund	48	49
OPM: Postal Service Retiree Health Benefits Fund	[d]	45
FDIC: The Deposit Insurance Fund	39	32
OPM: Employees Life Insurance Fund	39	40
DOT: Highway Trust Fund	24	14
OPM: Employees Health Benefits Fund	18	19
DOS: Foreign Service Retirement and Disability Fund	16	17
DOL: Pension Benefit Guaranty Corporation	15	15
DOL: Unemployment Trust Fund	12	16
NCUA: National Credit Union Share Insurance Fund	10	11
Total	**$3,673**	**$4,624**

Source: Monthly Statements of the Public Debt of the United States for April 30, 2011, and December 31, 2011.

[a]Social Security Administration (SSA), Department of Defense (DOD), Department of Health and Human Services (HHS), Department of Energy (DOE), Federal Deposit Insurance Corporation (FDIC), Office of Personnel Management (OPM), Department of Transportation (DOT), Department of State (DOS), Department of Labor (DOL), National Credit Union Administration (NCUA).

[b]These represent the reported holdings as of the month-end dates that immediately preceded Treasury's initiation of extraordinary actions.

[c]These are the Social Security trust funds.

[d]Treasury took extraordinary actions related to these funds during 2011 to manage federal debt when delays in raising the debt limit occurred. As such, normal investment and redemption policies and procedures were not followed for these funds.

[e]The CSRDF also held about $8 billion of FFB securities, which are not GAS securities. The reported balance of these securities remained the same throughout January 2012.

[f]These are the Medicare trust funds.

Treasury Restored Uninvested Principal and Interest Losses as Authorized

In accordance with relevant legislation and consistent with the timing of the debt limit increases authorized by the BCA, Treasury restored the uninvested principal amounts to the CSRDF, Postal Benefits Fund, and G-Fund, and invested the uninvested principal to the ESF totaling approximately $299.5 billion. This amount consisted of (1) $239.9 billion of uninvested principal relating to the period from May 16, 2011, through August 1, 2011,[19] and (2) $59.6 billion relating to the period in January 2012, in which Treasury took extraordinary actions to manage federal debt when delays in raising the debt limit occurred. In accordance with legislation, Treasury also restored interest losses totaling approximately $933.8 million to the CSRDF, Postal Benefits Fund, and G-Fund. This amount consisted of (1) $916.9 million relating to the period from May 16, 2011, through August 1, 2011, and (2) $16.9 million relating to the period in January 2012. Treasury lacks legislative authority under section 5302 of title 31, United States Code, to restore interest losses to the ESF. Table 4 summarizes the amounts of principal and interest restored.

Table 4: Restored Principal and Interest Related to Extraordinary Actions Taken to Manage Debt during 2011 and January 2012

Federal government accounts	2011		January 2012	
	Uninvested principal as of August 1, 2011	Interest losses from May 16-August 1, 2011	Uninvested principal as of January 27, 2012	Interest losses from January 4-27, 2012
CSRDF	$86.0 billion	$516.9 million	n/a	n/a
Postal Benefits Fund	$9.5 billion	$21.5 million	n/a	n/a
G-Fund	$137.5 billion	$378.5 million	$36.9 billion	$16.9 million
ESF	$6.9 billion[a]	[a]	$22.7 billion[a]	[a]
Total	$239.9 billion	$916.9 million	$59.6 billion	$16.9 million

Source: GAO analysis of documentation from Treasury.

[a]Section 5302 of title 31, United States Code, provides Treasury the authority to invest principal of the ESF. Treasury did not restore interest losses of $55,630 for 2011 and $284,691 for January 2012 relating to the ESF because it lacks legislative authority to do so under section 5302 of title 31, United States Code.

CSRDF and Postal Benefits Fund

Subsections 8348(j)(3) and (4) of title 5, United States Code, require Treasury to immediately restore, to the maximum extent practicable, the CSRDF's Treasury holdings to the proper balances when a DISP ends

---

[19]The investment of uninvested principal of $239.9 billion used a large portion of the $400 billion increase to the debt limit on August 2, 2011.

and to restore lost interest on the next normal interest payment date. Treasury is required by subsection 8909a(c) of title 5, United States Code, to follow these same procedures for the Postal Benefits Fund. Consequently, Treasury took the following actions, with respect to these two funds, once the DISP for 2011 had ended:

- Treasury invested about $86 billion of uninvested principal to the CSRDF on August 2, 2011, which equaled the amount of new investments suspended during 2011.
- All of the $17.1 billion of Treasury securities held by the CSRDF that Treasury redeemed earlier than normal had been used for CSRDF benefit payments and expenses during the DISP. As such, there was no remaining amount required to be invested.
- Treasury invested about $9.5 billion of uninvested principal to the Postal Benefits Fund on August 2, 2011, which equaled the amount of new investments suspended during 2011.
- On December 30, 2011, Treasury paid the CSRDF about $516.9 million and the Postal Benefits Fund about $21.5 million to restore interest losses incurred because of the actions Treasury had taken during the DISP. Because December 30, 2011, was the first semiannual interest payment date since the DISP ended, this was the proper restoration date according to the statute authorizing the restoration.

We verified that subsequent to the initiation and recording of these transactions, the CSRDF's and Postal Benefits Fund's holdings were, in effect, the same as they would have been had the DISP not occurred.

G-Fund

On August 1, 2011, and January 27, 2012, the last business days before the debt limit was raised, the G-Fund had uninvested principal of about $137.5 billion and $36.9 billion, respectively. On August 2, 2011, and January 30, 2012, Treasury invested all uninvested principal for the G-Fund, as required by subsection 8438(g)(3) of title 5, United States Code. Treasury is also required by subsection 8438(g)(4) of title 5, United States Code, to make the G-Fund whole by restoring any losses once the suspension of debt has ended. During May through August 2011 and January 2012, interest losses to the G-Fund were about $378.5 million and $16.9 million, respectively, because its funds were not fully invested. On August 3, 2011, and January 30, 2012, Treasury fully restored the lost interest on the G-Fund's uninvested funds. We verified that subsequent to the initiation and recording of these transactions, the G-Fund's holdings were, in effect, the same as they would have been had the suspensions of debt not occurred.

ESF

On August 1, 2011, and January 27, 2012, the last business days before the debt limit was raised, the ESF had uninvested principal of about $6.9 billion and $22.7 billion, respectively. On August 2, 2011, and January 30, 2012, Treasury invested all uninvested principal for the ESF. During May through August 2011 and January 2012, interest losses to the ESF were $55,630 and $284,691, respectively, because its funds were not fully invested. Treasury has the authority in section 5302 of title 31, United States Code, to invest principal of the ESF. However, the Secretary of the Treasury lacks legislative authority to restore any interest losses relating to the ESF incurred as a result of authorized actions taken by Treasury to manage federal debt when delays in raising the debt limit occur. We verified that Treasury properly invested the ESF's uninvested principal and, in accordance with the law, did not restore interest losses.

Delays in Raising the Debt Limit Increased Treasury's Borrowing Costs and Affected Its Operations

Congress usually votes on increasing the debt limit after fiscal policy decisions affecting federal borrowing have begun to take effect. Debt limit increases frequently involve lengthy debate, with the debates often occurring when federal debt is near or at the debt limit. We reported in February 2011 that managing debt when delays in raising the debt limit occur diverts Treasury's resources away from other cash and debt management responsibilities and that Treasury's borrowing costs modestly increased during debt limit debates in 2002, 2003, and 2010.[20] As discussed below, increased borrowing costs also occurred during 2011 when there was a delay in raising the debt limit. For the January 2012 period, we found that there was no consistent pattern of yield spread changes and the changes in borrowing costs were negligible. This was expected given that the BCA provided for a future debt limit increase, which minimized uncertainty in the Treasury market. In addition, managing federal debt during such delays affected Treasury's normal operations in 2011 and January 2012.

---

[20]GAO-11-203.

Treasury's Borrowing Costs on Certain Securities Increased When Delays in Raising the Debt Limit Occurred in 2011

Our analysis indicates that delays in raising the debt limit in 2011 led to increased borrowing costs on certain securities. We measured changes in Treasury's borrowing costs when delays in raising the debt limit occurred in 2011 using a multivariate regression analysis of the daily yield spread—yields on private securities minus yields on Treasury securities of comparable maturities—between the debt limit event period and the previous 3 months, or pre-event period. Rates for Treasury and other securities fluctuate from day to day in response to changes in the broader economy. Focusing on a yield spread rather than changes in individual interest rates facilitated the measurement of changes in the relative risk of Treasury securities and the identification of potential risk premiums (which is represented by a decrease in the yield spread). We also controlled for other factors that could affect the yield spread, such as the Federal Reserve's holdings of Treasury securities and economic uncertainty. (See app. II for more details on how we estimated increased borrowing costs.) The results of our multivariate regression analysis describe the change in yield spreads attributable to delays in raising the debt limit. The estimated increase or decrease in the yield spreads between the pre-event and event periods is shown in figure 2.

Figure 2: Estimated Increase or Decrease in Spreads between Private and Treasury Security Yields for the 2011 Debt Limit Event Period (January 6, 2011, through August 1, 2011)

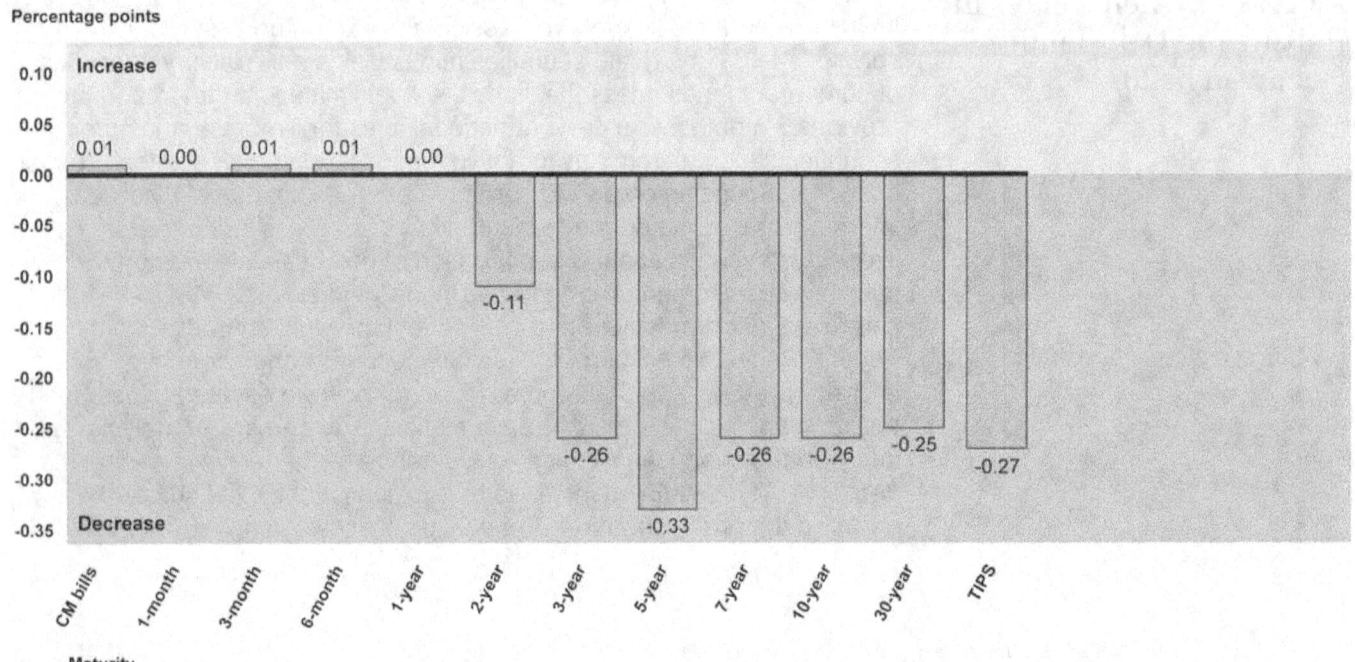

Source: GAO analysis of data from the Treasury, Federal Reserve Bank of St. Louis, and IHS Global Insight.

A decrease in the yield spread indicates that the market perceives the risk of Treasury securities to be closer to that of private securities, increasing the cost to Treasury. Conversely, an increase in the yield spread indicates that the market perceives the risk of Treasury securities to have decreased relative to that of private securities, making the securities less costly to Treasury. We found that the 2011 debt limit event led to a premium on Treasury securities with maturities of 2 years or more while Treasury securities with shorter maturities either experienced no change or became slightly less costly relative to private securities. Applying the relevant increase or decrease in the yield spread shown in figure 2 to all Treasury bills, notes, bonds, CM bills, and TIPS issued during the 2011 debt limit event period, we estimated that borrowing costs increased by about $1.3 billion in fiscal year 2011.[21] Many of the Treasury securities

---

[21]The 95 percent confidence interval of the borrowing cost estimate is about $1 billion to $1.7 billion.

issued during the 2011 debt limit event period will remain outstanding for years to come. Accordingly, the multiyear increase in borrowing costs arising from the event is greater than the additional borrowing costs during fiscal year 2011 alone.

There are limitations to using a multivariate regression to measure changes in Treasury's borrowing costs attributable to delays in raising the debt limit. Most important, many economic and financial developments besides the uncertainty in the Treasury market arising from delays in raising the debt limit likely affected yield spreads during this period. While we controlled for changes in Federal Reserve holdings of Treasury securities, stock market uncertainty, and economic activity, we cannot capture every development affecting yield spreads, such as other policy changes not easily quantifiable that might affect yield spreads.

Managing Debt When Delays in Raising the Debt Limit Occurred in 2011 and January 2012 Affected Treasury's Normal Operations

Debt and cash management required more time and Treasury resources as delays in raising the debt limit occurred in 2011 and January 2012. For example, Treasury staff (1) forecasted and monitored with increasing frequency and in increasing detail cash and borrowing needs and (2) developed, reviewed, and tested contingency plans and alternative scenarios for the possible implementation of extraordinary actions. According to Treasury officials, these activities diverted time and Treasury resources from other cash and debt management responsibilities. We reviewed estimates provided by the Office of Fiscal Projections (OFP) and the Bureau of the Public Debt (BPD), the entities primarily affected by the delays, which indicated that these entities' personnel devoted as much as several hundred hours per week to managing federal debt when delays in raising the debt limit occurred in 2011 and January 2012.

According to Treasury officials, for 2011, Treasury's operational focus on the debt limit began at least 6 months before the debt limit was expected to be reached and increased as debt neared the limit. Treasury's OFP staff developed estimates under multiple scenarios of when debt might reach the debt limit. As federal debt neared the debt limit, these estimates were developed weekly, then daily, and finally multiple times a day. According to Treasury officials, preparing these estimates, informing departmental officials, and other preparatory tasks were a critical focus of OFP's staff. To manage federal debt when delays in raising the debt limit occurred in 2011, Treasury officials estimated that OFP spent almost 15 staff hours per business day performing these tasks. In addition, Treasury officials estimated that OFP expended about 200 staff hours in total to prepare for and manage the extraordinary actions taken in January 2012.

BPD—the bureau within Treasury that is responsible for implementing the extraordinary actions and for the accounting associated with those transactions—also dedicated extensive resources to operations related to the debt limit. BPD estimated that managing federal debt when delays in raising the debt limit occurred in 2011 and January 2012 resulted in almost 5,750 hours of work, including over 400 hours of overtime and compensatory time. This included more than 1,200 hours in the weeks prior to the use of extraordinary actions for meetings, preparation of parallel accounts and spreadsheets to use in tracking uninvested principal and interest losses, tests of the accounting system, and training staff. The majority of time was spent implementing the extraordinary actions. BPD estimated that it spent almost 63 staff hours per business day on debt limit–related activities from May 16, 2011, through August 1, 2011, and almost 31 staff hours per business day from January 4, 2012, through January 27, 2012. After the debt limit was increased, BPD estimated that it spent over 500 hours on activities such as restoring uninvested funds and preparing reports.

Treasury officials said that the increased focus on debt limit–related operations in the months and weeks approaching the debt limit diverted time and attention from other cash and debt management tasks that could improve Treasury operations. For example, according to Treasury officials, OFP delayed participation in federal cash expenditure process modernization efforts and the development of a new fiscal forecasting system. Similarly, BPD officials said that they spent less time updating procedures for issuing debt to the public and modernizing debt accounting systems. According to these officials, these activities help Treasury more accurately project future borrowing needs and perform debt management activities more effectively. More accurately projecting future borrowing needs helps Treasury avoid (1) borrowing more than is needed to fund the government's immediate needs, which results in increased interest costs, and (2) borrowing less than is sufficient to maintain Treasury's operating cash balance at a minimum level through regularly scheduled issuances of marketable Treasury securities, which may require Treasury to issue CM bills with little advance notice to the market, resulting in potentially higher interest costs. Treasury officials also stated that they spent less time on staff development and program oversight activities to perform additional tasks needed to manage federal debt when delays in raising the debt limit occurred.

Concluding Observations

The extraordinary actions Treasury took during 2011 and January 2012 to manage federal debt when delays in raising the debt limit occurred were consistent with relevant authorizing legislation and regulations. However, delays in raising the debt limit can create uncertainty in the Treasury market and lead to higher borrowing costs. We estimated that delays in raising the debt limit in 2011 led to an increase in Treasury's borrowing costs of about $1.3 billion in fiscal year 2011. However, this does not account for the multiyear effects on increased costs for Treasury securities that will remain outstanding after fiscal year 2011. Further, managing federal debt as such delays occurred was complex, time-consuming, and technically challenging. According to Treasury officials, these events diverted Treasury's staff away from other important cash and debt management responsibilities as well as staff development and program oversight activities.

Congress usually votes on increasing the debt limit after fiscal policy decisions affecting federal borrowing have begun to take effect. This approach to raising the debt limit does not facilitate debate over specific tax or spending proposals and their effect on debt. In February 2011, we reported, and continue to believe, that Congress should consider ways to better link decisions about the debt limit with decisions about spending and revenue to avoid potential disruptions to the Treasury market and to help inform the fiscal policy debate in a timely way.

Agency Comments

We requested comments on a draft of this report from the Secretary of the Treasury. In providing oral comments on the draft, Treasury broadly agreed with the draft's conclusions, expressed appreciation for our efforts to estimate the monetary impact of delays in raising the debt limit on Treasury's borrowing costs, and also commented on the broader impact of delays in raising the debt limit on the economy, which was beyond the scope of our review. Treasury also provided technical comments, which we incorporated as appropriate.

We will send copies of this report to interested congressional committees, the Secretary of the Treasury, and other interested parties. In addition, the report is available at no charge on the GAO website at http://www.gao.gov.

If you or your staff have any questions about this report, please contact Gary T. Engel at (202) 512-3406 or engelg@gao.gov, Susan J. Irving at (202) 512-6806 or irvings@gao.gov, or Thomas J. McCool at (202) 512-2642 or mccoolt@gao.gov. Contact points for our Offices of Congressional Relations and Public Affairs may be found on the last page of this report. GAO staff who made major contributions to this report are listed in appendix III.

Gary T. Engel
Director
Financial Management and Assurance

Susan J. Irving
Director for Federal Budget Analysis
Strategic Issues

Thomas J. McCool
Director
Center for Economics, Applied Research and Methods

Appendix I: Objectives, Scope, and Methodology

With regard to actions taken by the Department of the Treasury (Treasury) during 2011 and January 2012 to manage federal debt when delays in raising the debt limit occurred, our objectives were to (1) provide a chronology of the significant events, (2) analyze whether actions taken by Treasury were consistent with legal authorities provided to manage federal debt during such delays, (3) assess the extent to which Treasury restored uninvested principal and interest losses to federal government accounts in accordance with relevant legislation, and (4) analyze the effect that delays in raising the debt limit had on Treasury's borrowing costs and operations.

To address the first objective, we reviewed congressional actions increasing the debt limit and Treasury correspondence, announcements, and documentation of the extraordinary actions taken. We reviewed letters sent by the Secretary of the Treasury to Congress requesting debt limit increases and discussing when Treasury's borrowing authority would be exhausted, and Treasury announcements of specific extraordinary actions. For each business day from May 16, 2011, through August 2, 2011, and January 4, 2012, through January 30, 2012, we reviewed correspondence from Treasury's Office of Fiscal Projections (OFP) to Treasury's Bureau of the Public Debt (BPD) providing specific instructions and timing of the extraordinary actions to be taken as well as BPD's documentation implementing the actions.

We performed the work for the second and third objectives as part of our financial audits of the fiscal years 2011 and 2012 Schedules of Federal Debt Managed by BPD.[1] To address the second objective, for each business day during the above-noted periods, we reviewed Treasury accounting documentation, including specific instructions from OFP to BPD, to verify that the extraordinary actions taken for the affected federal government accounts were consistent with relevant legislation. For suspensions of investments, we reviewed BPD documentation and verified that BPD only invested the amount instructed by OFP using the appropriate security type and date. For the one Civil Service Retirement and Disability Fund (CSRDF) security that was redeemed earlier than normal, we reviewed BPD documentation and verified that BPD processed it for the amount, security type, and date as instructed by OFP.

---

[1]GAO, *Financial Audit: Bureau of the Public Debt's Fiscal Years 2011 and 2010 Schedules of Federal Debt*, GAO-12-164 (Washington, D.C.: Nov. 8, 2011).

For State and Local Government Series (SLGS) securities, we reviewed Treasury documentation of actions taken to suspend new issuances and convert SLGS demand deposit securities and compared those actions taken to authorizing regulations.

Over 230 federal government accounts have the authority or the requirement to invest excess receipts in Treasury securities, and Treasury officials stated that normal investment and redemption policies and procedures were used for all but 4 of these accounts for 2011 and 2 of these accounts for January 2012. To evaluate whether Treasury followed normal investment and redemption policies and procedures for federal government accounts not affected by the extraordinary actions, we selected for review accounts with balances greater than $10 billion as of April 30, 2011 (15 accounts) and December 31, 2011 (17 accounts). As of both dates, this represented about 97 percent of the reported total of Treasury securities held by the federal government accounts not affected by the extraordinary actions. We obtained investment and redemption activity files from BPD for these accounts and performed the following audit procedures:

- Reviewed trends in daily investment and redemption activity and compared these trends to prior year trends to determine whether there were any unusual fluctuations.
- Selected and reviewed investment and redemption transactions greater than $5 billion from May 16, 2011, through August 1, 2011, and January 4, 2012, through January 27, 2012, to determine whether the transactions were processed in accordance with Treasury's normal policies and procedures. The selected transactions for the 2011 and 2012 periods represented about 86 percent and 78 percent, respectively, of the total investment transactions, and 81 percent and 80 percent, respectively, of the total redemption transactions.
- Confirmed with personnel from the respective agencies the total amount of investments and redemptions reported by Treasury from May 16, 2011, through August 1, 2011.[2]

---

[2]We determined that it was not necessary to perform this step for the January 2012 period of managing federal debt when delays in raising the debt limit occurred because the risks associated with this period were minimal. Specifically, the January 2012 period lasted 17 business days and Treasury only used a small portion of the extraordinary actions available.

We also reviewed Treasury reports of fund balances for federal
government accounts with investment authority to identify any large
positive uninvested balances, which would indicate that normal policies
and procedures were not being followed, as of the end of the month for
May through September 2011, December 2011, and January 2012.

To address the third objective, we reviewed BPD schedules and parallel
accounts of uninvested principal and forgone interest for the CSRDF,
Postal Service Retiree Health Benefits Fund, Government Securities
Investment Fund of the Federal Employees' Retirement System, and
Exchange Stabilization Fund. We recalculated the cumulative uninvested
principal as of August 1, 2011, and January 27, 2012, and compared our
calculations to BPD restoration entries. We also recalculated the forgone
interest on these uninvested principal amounts and compared our
calculations to BPD's interest restoration entries. We reviewed accounting
documentation of Treasury actions to restore uninvested principal and
interest and compared these actions to relevant legislation.

To address the fourth objective, we performed a multivariate regression
analysis of the daily yield spread—yields on private securities minus
yields on Treasury securities of comparable maturities—during the 2011
debt limit event period. We used yield spreads during the 3-month pre-
event period as a benchmark against which yield spreads during the
event period were compared. We also examined changes in the yield
spread during the January 2012 debt limit event period. See appendix II
for more details on how we estimated increased borrowing costs,
including limitations to our using a multivariate regression to measure
changes in Treasury's borrowing costs attributable to delays in raising the
debt limit. We obtained Treasury auction data for this analysis from
Treasury. We obtained data on security yields, the Federal Reserve's
holdings of Treasury securities, and the Chicago Board Options
Exchange's Volatility Index from the Federal Reserve Bank of St. Louis's
Federal Reserve Economic Data (FRED) source. FRED includes original
source data from the Federal Reserve Board, Bank of America Merrill
Lynch, the British Bankers Association, and the Chicago Board Options
Exchange. We also used data on Standard & Poor's 500 total return
index from IHS Global Insight in our analysis. To assess the reliability of
these data, we looked for outliers and anomalies. These databases are
commonly used by Treasury and researchers to examine the Treasury
market and related transactions. On the basis of our assessment, we
believe the data are sufficiently reliable for the purpose of this review.

To understand how managing debt affected agency operations when delays in raising the debt limit occurred in 2011 and January 2012, we reviewed documents provided by Treasury, interviewed Treasury officials involved in the decision-making process and implementation of the extraordinary actions, and obtained estimates of the number of personnel and amount of time involved in managing debt during such delays. To assess the reasonableness of Treasury's estimates, we reviewed e-mails, memos, press releases, written procedures, accounting documentation, and other corroborating information prepared by OFP and BPD. However, we did not obtain sufficient supporting documentation to independently verify Treasury's staff hour estimates. We were also unable to independently verify the forgone opportunities that Treasury identified, such as less time for other cash and debt management tasks that could improve Treasury operations, in part because it is difficult to prove what would have happened in the absence of the delay in raising the debt limit.

We conducted this performance audit from May 2011 to July 2012 in accordance with generally accepted government auditing standards. Those standards require that we plan and perform the audit to obtain sufficient, appropriate evidence to provide a reasonable basis for our findings and conclusions based on our audit objectives. We believe that the evidence obtained provides a reasonable basis for our findings and conclusions based on our audit objectives.

Appendix II: Detailed Methodology Used to Analyze Effect on Treasury's Borrowing Costs

To measure changes in Treasury's borrowing costs when delays in raising the debt limit occurred in 2011, we performed a multivariate regression analysis of the daily yield spread—yields on private securities minus yields on Treasury securities of comparable maturities—during the debt limit event period.[1] For our purposes, the 2011 debt limit event began with the January 6, 2011, letter from the Secretary of the Treasury notifying the Senate Majority Leader that the debt limit needed to be raised and ended August 1, 2011, the business day prior to the debt limit increase.

We used daily yield spreads during the 3-month pre-event period as a benchmark against which yield spreads during the event period were compared. A decrease in the yield spread indicates that the market perceives the risk of Treasury securities to be closer to that of private securities, increasing the cost to Treasury. Conversely, an increase in the yield spread indicates that the market perceives the risk of Treasury securities to have decreased relative to that of private securities, making the securities less costly to Treasury. We assumed that Treasury Inflation-Protected Securities experienced the same yield spread changes as nominal securities with similar maturities and that any change in inflation expectations during the debt limit event should have equal effects on private securities and Treasury nominal securities. Our results indicate that the 2011 debt limit event period led to a premium (which is represented by a decrease in the yield spread) ranging from 11 to 33 basis points on Treasury securities with maturities of 2 or more years.[2] For 3-month and 6-month Treasury bills and cash management bills, which typically had a maturity of 56 days, the debt limit event period led to a 1 basis point decline in Treasury yields relative to private security yields during the period (which is represented by an increase in the yield spread), while there was no change in yields on 1-month and 1-year Treasury bills relative to private security yields. Overall, Treasury yields

---

[1]During the January 2012 debt limit event period, which began with the use of the first extraordinary action on January 4, 2012, and ended January 27, 2012, the business day prior to the debt limit increase, there was no consistent pattern of yield spread changes and the changes in borrowing costs were negligible. Accordingly, we did not perform a multivariate regression of the yield spread.

[2]A basis point is equal to 1/100th of 1 percent. Thus, 11 basis points is 0.11 percent.

increased relative to comparable-maturity private securities during the 2011 debt limit event period.[3]

The existing literature on the effect of the debt limit on Treasury's borrowing costs is limited. Previous analysis has focused mainly on the effect of debt limit events on short-term Treasury interest rates. In an analysis we replicated and updated, Liu, Shao, and Yeager (2009)[4] found that during debt limit events in 2001-2002 and 2002-2003, the spread between 3-month Treasury bill yields and 3-month commercial paper yields narrowed, implying that Treasury bills were relatively more costly during this period; however, this relationship was not observed in either the 2004-2005 or 2005-2006 debt limit events. The authors hypothesized that during these latter two debt limit events, investors may have assumed based on past experience that Members of Congress would resolve their differences before there were any serious disruptions in the Treasury market and therefore did not charge a premium on securities issued during the debt limit event. Our 2011 report replicated the authors' analysis and also found that the 2009-2010 debt limit event coincided with a 4 basis point increase in 3-month Treasury bill yields.[5] An earlier study by Nippani, Liu, and Schulman found that Treasury paid a premium on 3-month and 6-month Treasury bills issued during the debt limit event in 1995-1996.[6]

Our analysis of Treasury's borrowing costs around past debt limit events focused on 3-month Treasury bills, consistent with the approach used in past studies. However, because uncertainty could affect all Treasury securities, we expanded our analysis of the 2011-2012 debt limit events to cover yields on longer-term securities as well. For the 2011 debt limit

---

[3]A test of statistical significance attempts to rule out an effect purely attributable to chance. The coefficient for the event was significant at the 95 percent level for all maturities except for 1-month and 1-year securities, which displayed no statistically significant change in the yield spread. A 95 percent significance level means that there is less than a 5 percent probability of rejecting the null hypothesis that the coefficient is zero when the null hypothesis is true.

[4]Pu Liu, Yingying Shao, and Timothy J. Yeager, "Did the repeated debt ceiling controversies embed default risk in U.S. Treasury securities?" *Journal of Banking and Finance*, vol. 33 (8) (2009): 1464-1471.

[5]GAO-11-203.

[6]Srinivas Nippani, Pu Liu, and Craig T. Schulman, "Are Treasury Securities Free of Default?" *Journal of Financial and Quantitative Analysis*, vol. 36, no. 2 (2001): 251-265.

event, we estimated a regression explaining the private-Treasury yield spread for each maturity range using a constant term, dummy variables for the event and postevent periods,[7] Federal Reserve holdings of Treasury securities, the Chicago Board Options Exchange's Volatility Index[8] to capture financial market uncertainty, and the daily percentage change in the Standard & Poor's 500 total return index to capture economic activity.

Effect of Delayed Increase in the Debt Limit on Treasury's Borrowing Costs

On the basis of our analysis, we estimated that delays in raising the debt limit in 2011 led to an increase in Treasury's borrowing costs of about $1.3 billion in fiscal year 2011.[9] We derived this estimate by multiplying the amount of Treasury securities issued at each maturity during the event period by regression-based estimates of the relevant yield spread change attributable to the debt limit event and weighting the result by the portion of fiscal year 2011 during which the security was outstanding. Many of the Treasury securities issued during the 2011 debt limit event will remain outstanding for years to come. Accordingly, the multiyear increase in borrowing costs arising from the event is greater than the additional borrowing costs during fiscal year 2011 alone.

Limitations of the Analysis

There are limitations to using a multivariate regression to measure changes in Treasury's borrowing costs attributable to delays in raising the debt limit. Most important, many economic and financial developments besides the uncertainty in the Treasury market arising from delays in raising the debt limit likely affected yield spreads during this period. While we controlled for changes in Federal Reserve holdings of Treasury securities, financial market uncertainty, and economic activity, we cannot capture every development affecting yield spreads, such as other policy changes that are not easily quantifiable that might affect yield spreads.

---

[7]Consistent with the approach used in past studies, the 2011 postevent period was for the 90-day period from August 2, 2011.

[8]This variable represents the market expectations of volatility over the next 30-day period and is calculated by the Chicago Board Options Exchange using Standard & Poor's 500 stock index option bid/ask quotes. The variable is intended to control for volatility and uncertainty in financial markets.

[9]The 95 percent confidence interval of the borrowing cost estimate is about $1 billion to $1.7 billion.

Appendix III: GAO Contacts and Staff Acknowledgments

GAO Contacts	Gary T. Engel, (202) 512-3406 or engelg@gao.gov Susan J. Irving, (202) 512-6806 or irvings@gao.gov Thomas J. McCool, (202) 512-2642 or mccoolt@gao.gov
Staff Acknowledgments	In addition to the contacts named above, Richard S. Krashevski, Dawn B. Simpson, and Melissa A. Wolf, Assistant Directors; Carolyn M. Voltz, Analyst-in-Charge; Nicole X. Dow; Brian S. Harechmak; Dervla Carmen Harris; Thomas J. McCabe; and Shaundell A. Williams made key contributions to this report.

www.ingramcontent.com/pod-product-compliance
Lightning Source LLC
Chambersburg PA
CBHW080931290526
45795CB00007BA/2701